LAYERS OF LEARNING

YEAR THREE • UNIT FOURTEEN

SLAVE TRADE
BRAZIL
GEMS & MINERALS
COLONIAL ART

Published by HooDoo Publishing
United States of America
© 2015 Layers of Learning

UNITS AT A GLANCE: TOPICS FOR ALL FOUR YEARS OF THE LAYERS OF LEARNING PROGRAM

1	History	Geography	Science	The Arts
1	Mesopotamia	Maps & Globes	Planets	Cave Paintings
2	Egypt	Map Keys	Stars	Egyptian Art
3	Europe	Global Grids	Earth & Moon	Crafts
4	Ancient Greece	Wonders	Satellites	Greek Art
5	Babylon	Mapping People	Humans in Space	Poetry
6	The Levant	Physical Earth	Laws of Motion	List Poems
7	Phoenicians	Oceans	Motion	Moral Stories
8	Assyrians	Deserts	Fluids	Rhythm
9	Persians	Arctic	Waves	Melody
10	Ancient China	Forests	Machines	Chinese Art
11	Early Japan	Mountains	States of Matter	Line & Shape
12	Arabia	Rivers & Lakes	Atoms	Color & Value
13	Ancient India	Grasslands	Elements	Texture & Form
14	Ancient Africa	Africa	Bonding	African Tales
15	First North Americans	North America	Salts	Creative Kids
16	Ancient South America	South America	Plants	South American Art
17	Celts	Europe	Flowering Plants	Jewelry
18	Roman Republic	Asia	Trees	Roman Art
19	Christianity	Australia & Oceania	Simple Plants	Instruments
20	Roman Empire	You Explore	Fungi	Composing Music

2	History	Geography	Science	The Arts
1	Byzantines	Turkey	Climate & Seasons	Byzantine Art
2	Barbarians	Ireland	Forecasting	Illumination
3	Islam	Arabian Peninsula	Clouds & Precipitation	Creative Kids
4	Vikings	Norway	Special Effects	Viking Art
5	Anglo Saxons	Britain	Wild Weather	King Arthur Tales
6	Charlemagne	France	Cells and DNA	Carolingian Art
7	Normans	Nigeria	Skeletons	Canterbury Tales
8	Feudal System	Germany	Muscles, Skin, & Cardiopulmonary	Gothic Art
9	Crusades	Balkans	Digestive & Senses	Religious Art
10	Burgundy, Venice, Spain	Switzerland	Nerves	Oil Paints
11	Wars of the Roses	Russia	Health	Minstrels & Plays
12	Eastern Europe	Hungary	Metals	Printmaking
13	African Kingdoms	Mali	Carbon Chem	Textiles
14	Asian Kingdoms	Southeast Asia	Non-metals	Vivid Language
15	Mongols	Caucasus	Gases	Fun With Poetry
16	Medieval China & Japan	China	Electricity	Asian Arts
17	Pacific Peoples	Micronesia	Circuits	Arts of the Islands
18	American Peoples	Canada	Technology	Indian Legends
19	The Renaissance	Italy	Magnetism	Renaissance Art I
20	Explorers	Caribbean Sea	Motors	Renaissance Art II

3	History	Geography	Science	The Arts
1	Age of Exploration	Argentina and Chile	Classification & Insects	Fairy Tales
2	The Ottoman Empire	Egypt and Libya	Reptiles & Amphibians	Poetry
3	Mogul Empire	Pakistan & Afghanistan	Fish	Mogul Arts
4	Reformation	Angola & Zambia	Birds	Reformation Art
5	Renaissance England	Tanzania & Kenya	Mammals & Primates	Shakespeare
6	Thirty Years' War	Spain	Sound	Baroque Music
7	The Dutch	Netherlands	Light & Optics	Baroque Art I
8	France	Indonesia	Bending Light	Baroque Art II
9	The Enlightenment	Korean Pen.	Color	Art Journaling
10	Russia & Prussia	Central Asia	History of Science	Watercolors
11	Conquistadors	Baltic States	Igneous Rocks	Creative Kids
12	Settlers	Peru & Bolivia	Sedimentary Rocks	Native American Art
13	13 Colonies	Central America	Metamorphic Rocks	Settler Sayings
14	Slave Trade	Brazil	Gems & Minerals	Colonial Art
15	The South Pacific	Australasia	Fossils	Principles of Art
16	The British in India	India	Chemical Reactions	Classical Music
17	Boston Tea Party	Japan	Reversible Reactions	Folk Music
18	Founding Fathers	Iran	Compounds & Solutions	Rococo
19	Declaring Independence	Samoa and Tonga	Oxidation & Reduction	Creative Crafts I
20	The American Revolution	South Africa	Acids & Bases	Creative Crafts II

4	History	Geography	Science	The Arts
1	American Government	USA	Heat & Temperature	Patriotic Music
2	Expanding Nation	Pacific States	Motors & Engines	Tall Tales
3	Industrial Revolution	U.S. Landscapes	Energy	Romantic Art I
4	Revolutions	Mountain West States	Energy Sources	Romantic Art II
5	Africa	U.S. Political Maps	Energy Conversion	Impressionism I
6	The West	Southwest States	Earth Structure	Impressionism II
7	Civil War	National Parks	Plate Tectonics	Post-Impressionism
8	World War I	Plains States	Earthquakes	Expressionism
9	Totalitarianism	U.S. Economics	Volcanoes	Abstract Art
10	Great Depression	Heartland States	Mountain Building	Kinds of Art
11	World War II	Symbols and Landmarks	Chemistry of Air & Water	War Art
12	Modern East Asia	The South States	Food Chemistry	Modern Art
13	India's Independence	People of America	Industry	Pop Art
14	Israel	Appalachian States	Chemistry of Farming	Modern Music
15	Cold War	U.S. Territories	Chemistry of Medicine	Free Verse
16	Vietnam War	Atlantic States	Food Chains	Photography
17	Latin America	New England States	Animal Groups	Latin American Art
18	Civil Rights	Home State Study	Instincts	Theater & Film
19	Technology	Home State Study II	Habitats	Architecture
20	Terrorism	America in Review	Conservation	Creative Kids

Unit 3-14

Printable Pack

This unit includes printables at the end. To make life easier for you we also created digital printable packs for each unit. To retrieve your printable pack for Unit 3-1, please visit

www.layers-of-learning.com/digital-printable-packs/

Put the printable pack in your shopping cart and use this coupon code:

630UNIT3-14

Your printable pack will be free.

LAYERS OF LEARNING INTRODUCTION

This is part of a series of units in the Layers of Learning homeschool curriculum, including the subjects of history, geography, science, and the arts. Children from 1st through 12th can participate in the same curriculum at the same time - family school style.

The units are intended to be used in order as the basis of a complete curriculum (once you add in a systematic math, reading, and writing program). You begin with Year 1 Unit 1 no matter what ages your children are. Spend about 2 weeks on each unit. You pick and choose the activities within the unit that appeal to you and read the books from the book list that are available to you or find others on the same topic from your library. We highly recommend that you use the timeline in every history section as the backbone. Then flesh out your learning with reading and activities that highlight the topics you think are the most important.

Alternatively, you can use the units as activity ideas to supplement another curriculum in any order you wish. You can still use them with all ages of children at the same time.

When you've finished with Year One, move on to Year Two, Year Three, and Year Four. Then begin again with Year One and work your way through the years again. Now your children will be older, reading more involved books, and writing more in depth. When you have completed the sequence for the second time, you start again on it for the third and final time. If your student began with Layers of Learning in 1st grade and stayed with it all the way through she would go through the four year rotation three times, firmly cementing the information in her mind in ever increasing depth. At each level you should expect increasing amounts of outside reading and writing. High schoolers in particular should be reading extensively, and if possible, participating in discussion groups.

☺ ☻ ☻ These icons will guide you in spotting activities and books that are appropriate for the age of child you are working with. But if you think an activity is too juvenile or too difficult for your kids, adjust accordingly. The icons are not there as rules, just guides.

☺ GRADES 1-4

☻ GRADES 5-8

☻ GRADES 9-12

Within each unit we share:
- EXPLORATIONS, activities relating to the topic;
- EXPERIMENTS, usually associated with science topics;
- EXPEDITIONS, field trips;
- EXPLANATIONS, teacher helps or educational philosophies.

In the sidebars we also include Additional Layers, Famous Folks, Fabulous Facts, On the Web, and other extra related topics that can take you off on tangents, exploring the world and your interests with a bit more freedom. The curriculum will always be there to pull you back on track when you're ready.

You can learn more about how to use this curriculum at www.layers-of-learning.com/layers-of-learning-program/.

UNIT FOURTEEN
SLAVE TRADE – BRAZIL – MINERALS & GEMS – COLONIAL ART

For to be free is not merely to cast off one's chains, but to live in a way that respects and enhances the freedom of others.
-Nelson Mandela

LIBRARY LIST:

HISTORY

Search for: slave trade, American slavery, slavery, Toussaint L'Ouverture

☺ Amazing Grace: The Story of the Hymn by Linda Granfield. The author of the hymn was a slave trader, the most foul and evil of any profession at the time. But then his heart changed. This is the story of the slave trade and how it ended.

☺ If You Lived When There Was Slavery In America by Anne Kamma.

☺ Slavery: Real People and Their Stories of Enslavement by DK Publishing.

☺ A Picture Book of Frederick Douglass by David A. Adler.

☺ Now Let Me Fly: The Story of a Slave Family by Dolores Johnson.

☺ My Name is Phyllis Wheatley: A Story of Slavery and Freedom by Afua Cooper.

☺ ☻ The Story of Slavery by Sarah Courtauld. From ancient times to the present.

☻ Amos Fortune: Free Man by Elizabeth Yates. Fictionalized true story of an African king captured and brought to North America.

☻ To Be a Slave by Julius Lester. Firsthand accounts from people who were slaves in the Americas.

☻ Chains by Laurie Halse Anderson. A teenage slave girl spies on her loyalist masters during the revolutionary war in an effort to achieve her own freedom. Fictional.

☻ ☻ The Slave Dancer by Paula Fox. A young boy is kidnapped from the wharves of New Orleans and forced to play his flute while slaves dance to keep them in shape to be sold. A difficult book, read it first to be sure it's appropriate for your middle grader.

☻ ☻ Egalite for All: Toussaint Louverture and the Haitian Revolution, a PBS Home DVD.

☻ Amazing Grace by Eric Metaxes. The story of William Wilberforce and his fight to end the slave trade.

☻ Amistad by David Pesci. Tells the story of a revolt on a slave ship and how the American legal system dealt with it. (Look for simplified versions for young kids).

☻ Narrative of the Life of Frederick Douglass by Frederick Douglass. A young slave grows up in America and eventually frees himself. A classic, read this if you skip everything else.

☻ The Slave Trade: The Story of the Atlantic Slave Trade 1440 – 1870 by Hugh Thomas. Very fat (900 pgs.), but very thorough and eye opening.

☻ White Cargo: The Forgotten History of Britain's White Slaves in America by Don Jordan and Michael Walsh. Disturbing, please pre-read before giving to your teen.

GEOGRAPHY	Search for: Brazil ☺ B is for Brazil by Maria de Fatimo Campos. An ABC book about Brazil and what you'll see there. ☺ Dancing Turtle: A Folk Tale From Brazil by Pleasant DeSpain and David Boston. This folktale was told by indigenous Brazilian people and spread all over South America. ☺ 1, 2, 3, Suddenly in Brazil: The Ribbons of Bonfim by Christina Falcon Moldonado. This is part of a series of books in which Martin's grandpa has provided a magical means for Martin to instantly travel all over the world and explore various countries. ☺ ☻ Brazil by Tara Walters. A New True Book that will teach you all about Brazil. ☺ ☻ Brazil by Emma Lynch. Part of the "We're From" series. You'll meet three Brazilian kids who introduce you to their country. ☻ Brazil in Pictures by Thomas Streissguth. This is part of an excellent series on countries around the world. It is much more in depth than the basic geography books for younger kids.
SCIENCE	Search for: gems, precious stones, birthstones, minerals ☺ ☻ ☻ Smithsonian Handbooks: Gemstones by Cally Hall. This guide would be a valuable supplement to a study of gems for any age. ☺ ☻ ☻ Gemstones of the World: Newly Revised Fifth Edition by Walter Shumann. Another excellent guide. Includes where various gems come from on the earth and lots of information about each gem. ☺ ☻ ☻ DK Eyewitness Books: Crystal and Gem by R.F. Symes and R.R. Harding. A classic DK-style book that works for kids all the way up through adults. ☺ National Geographic Kids Everything Rocks and Minerals: Dazzling Gems of Photos and Info That Will Rock Your World by Steve Tomecek. In National Geographic style, this book is visual and colorful and kids will love it. ☺ National Geographic Readers: Rocks and Minerals by Kathleen Weidner Zoefeld. ☺ ☻ Rocks and Minerals: A Gem of a Book by Simon Basher and Dan Green.
THE ARTS	Search for: colonial art, colonial architecture, John Singleton Copley, Benjamin West, Gilbert Stuart, Charles Willson Peale, (this is a hard to find subject) ☺ ☻ ☻ American Colonial: Puritan Simplicity to Georgian Grace by Wendell Garrett. The focus of this book is on architecture. ☺ Come Look With Me: Art in Early America by Randy Osofsky. ☺ ☻ The Silversmiths by Leonard Everett Fisher. Explains the art of colonial silversmiths. ☺ ☻ The Potters by Leonard Everett Fisher. ☺ ☻ Colonial Crafts by Bobbie Kalman. ☺ ☻ Colonial American Craftspeople by Bernardine S. Stevens. Out of print, look for used copies or in your library.

HISTORY: SLAVE TRADE

John Hawkins was a sea captain who pioneered English involvement in the Atlantic slave trade in the 16th century. Hawkins was the first Englishman to deport Africans from the west coast of Africa for sale in the West Indies. From the 17th century, Britain became a master in the trade in human cargo.

Writer's Workshop

Sadly, John Hawkins' crest was a bound slave. Design a crest that would represent you if you were an adventuring sea captain.

Slavery has been a condition of the human world since ancient times and occurred in nearly every culture all across the globe. At some point or other, every race has been held captive by every other. So the events of the 1600's and 1700's in the trading of human flesh were not new at all; in fact, they were the norm. In the 1500's Spanish colonies in the New World were well established. Most of the Europeans who came to South and Central America expected to be landowners and not laborers. They needed a source of cheap labor, and so they began to import slaves from Africa. Slaves were almost Africa's only export.

This is a painting of slaves on a Brazilian sugar plantation.

Over the course of the next three hundred years an estimated 13 million West Africans would be shipped across the Atlantic and sold as slaves in the New World. By far the largest number ended up on plantations and mines in South America or the Caribbean. About 388,000 Africans were shipped to the British Colonies in North America, only about 3 percent of the total. Africans were the target slaves for several reasons.

1. They were not Christians and therefore fair game (in the minds of the people of the time).
2. They were inexpensive, bought cheaply from other Africans or, more rarely, captured by European raids.
3. Ships crossing the Atlantic from the east to the west would otherwise have no cargo in many cases.
4. Africa was relatively close to the Americas, as opposed to Asia or the Pacific Isles.
5. Africans were more hardy, able to work in hot climates better

than the native Indian tribes.

6. Their dark skin and unfamiliar traditions made them easy to classify as sub-human and therefore eased the consciences of the Europeans.

7. Africa was a conglomerate of scattered tribes rather than consisting of powerful nation states, and the tribes did not have the power to protect their own people from the slavers.

"The Slave Ship" by J.M.W. Turner (1840), shows slaves being thrown overboard during an epidemic aboard ship. Insurance companies only paid for the slaves who were drowned at sea, not for those who died aboard of other causes, creating some horrific unintended consequences. The painting is a protest work and was displayed in London.

From 1777 to 1804 slavery was outlawed in the northern states of America, but it persisted in the South, with its economy built on slave labor until the conclusion of the Civil War in 1865. Meanwhile in Britain, William Wilberforce was changing the whole way slavery was viewed. Africans were finally being seen as people with all the rights and dignities accorded to human beings. In 1807 the slave trade was banned by England. England began to use its considerable fire power at sea to force the end of the slave trade. They also forced African nations to sign treaties ending the slave trade. More than one uncooperative African king was deposed in favor of someone who would end slavery. Other nations eventually followed England's example.

🙂 🙂 🙂 EXPLORATION: Timeline

You'll find printable timeline squares at the end of this unit.

• c. 1500 Portugal begins trading in slaves, mostly sending them

---

Additional Layer

Africa lost millions of its population not only to European slave traders, but also to Muslim slave traders who shipped slaves across the Sahara, the Indian Ocean, and up the Red Sea.

Additional Layer

We know that Africans in Africa enslaved other Africans all the time, but African slavery was not the same as European slavery of Africans. In some ways it was better and in other ways much much worse. Find out what it was like for a slave in Africa.

Fabulous Fact

During this same time period, the 19th century, 1.5 million Christians were kidnapped and enslaved by Muslims in Algiers and other places along the North African coast. But unlike Africa, their countrymen were not complicit and did come to their rescue, militarily subduing the Muslims.

Additional Layer

The Ashanti Kingdom of Africa is one example of a state that gained great wealth through the slave trade. The Ashanti greatly expanded their borders and, in the process of making war on their neighbors, they took many enemy slaves. Selling these slaves to the Europeans was very lucrative, so making war on neighbors became a business venture as well as a political one. Learn more about the Ashanti.

This is Elmina Castle in Ghana. Ashanti slaves were brought here to be sold to the Europeans in exchange for guns, rum, cloth, and metal tools.

Photo by Rijksdienst voor het Cultureel Erfgoed , CC license, Wikimedia.

Writer's Workshop

Is there still slavery in the world today? See if you can find out where and what forms modern slavery takes.

Write about how slavery can still exist even when it is illegal. How can it be combated?

to Brazil.
- 1562 Britain begins its African slave trade
- 1570 Portuguese establish colony in Angola
- 1680-1780 Peak of the Atlantic slave trade
- 1700-1717 Asante Empire is unified and participates heavily in slave trade in exchange for firearms
- 1789 Equiano writes his biography as a slave
- 1790's Abolitionist movement gains strength in Britain
- 1791 Haitian coup leaves a former slave, Toussaint L'Ouverture, in charge
- 1792 Denmark stops its slave trade
- 1794 France emancipates all slaves in her American colonies
- 1794 Slave ships are outlawed in the United States
- 1803 Dutch ban the slave trade
- 1804 Slavery is illegal in the northern United States
- 1804 Black Republic formed in Haiti
- 1807 British ban the slave trade
- 1815 Britain pressures Spain and Portugal into signing a treaty to phase out the slave trade
- 1820 U.S. declares slave trade a form of piracy, punishable by death; U.S. navy ships are dispatched to enforce this
- 1822 African Colonization Society forms in the U.S. to create a free republic in Africa (Liberia) for freed former slaves
- 1831 Slave revolt breaks out in Jamaica and is brutally suppressed, leading to swift emancipation by British parliament in England
- 1833 Britain emancipates its West Indian slaves
- 1836 Portugal bans the slave trade
- 1839 Amistad revolt erupts into new discussions on the legality and morality of slavery in the U.S.
- 1865 Slavery is illegal throughout all of the United States
- 1888 Slavery is illegal throughout the Americas

☺ ☻ EXPLORATION: Discussion

After doing some reading, discuss with your kids the moral issues of slavery. Why is it wrong? Who says it's wrong? Read the Declaration of Independence, which declares that "all men are created equal." What reason does the Declaration of Independence give for these "self-evident rights" of all mankind?

What does your own religious or moral tradition teach about how we should treat others and the value of humans?

American Southerners were devoutly Christian, which religion teaches expressly against such things as slavery. How did they justify what they were doing? What did the breaking of this moral law do to the characters and the souls of those who engaged in it? (*Uncle Tom's Cabin* and *Narrative of the Life of Frederick Douglass* particularly deal with this issue.)

☺ ☻**EXPLORATION: Slavery and Trade**
Study and discuss this map showing the Atlantic trade routes of the 17th century. What does it reveal? Write about what you see on the map and then share and discuss your findings.

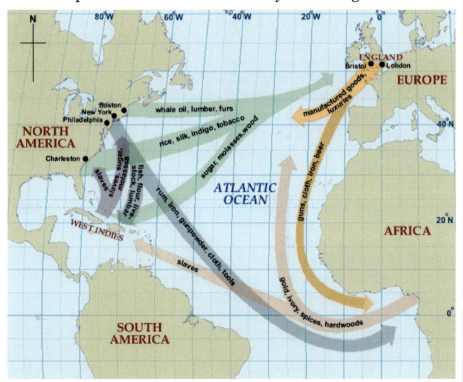

The British East India company brought goods to Africa where they were sold for slaves and the slaves in turn were brought to the Americas where they were sold for raw goods, such as cotton, tobacco, sugar, indigo, and other goods. These goods were taken to England where they were refined or processed and then sold all over Europe and the Americas. Tea and spices were also sold in Europe and the Americas. The tea spilled in Boston Harbor in 1773 was from India and the sale of it supported the British East India Company, which owned the majority of the slave ships. The British Empire was literally run on slavery. You can see why it was so hard to change the laws in England, especially when you realize that most members of parliament were part owners of the British East India Company.

☻**EXPLORATION: The African Response**
Africans were the ones enslaving other Africans, often their own countrymen and women, to trade to the Europeans for cloth,

Additional Layer

Research more about what the American founders thought about slavery.

This article does a good job explaining the evolving attitudes about slavery that the American colonists experienced as they struggled for their own freedom from Britain. http://www.wallbuilders. com/libissuesarticles.asp ?id=99

Additional Layer

Learn more about lives of slaves in the South. What was it like? Why did Southerners want slaves so badly?

Additional Layer

Slavery ended not because of government, but because of the opinion of the people in various nations. Discuss how the people have power to change things when they don't like how it's going.

Are there things you would like to change? Have there been any recent social changes brought about by changing public opinions? Are these changes always positive, or can they be morally, intellectually, or socially harmful as well?

Fabulous Fact

Maafa means "holocaust" or "great disaster" in Swahili, a term that African and African-American scholars use to describe the Atlantic Slave Trade.

Famous Folks

Queen Nzinga of Angola, though of doubtful personal character, fought successfully against the Portuguese to protect her people from the slave trade.

On the Web

This is a 46 minute documentary about the Middle Passage. Watch this with your kids, middle grades and up. https://youtu.be/yvhKeJ6m3rY

This video highlights that Africans had strong family structures. How did slavery destroy the family?

rum, muskets and other manufactured goods. But many Africans understood the injustice and the practical problems of the depopulation of African countries and tried to do something about it, though without the support of the European powers involved there was little they could do. Here is a letter from King Afonso I of Kongo to King João of Portugal in 1526 explaining part of the problem and hoping for some help from their trading partner.

And we cannot reckon how great the damage is, since the mentioned merchants are taking every day our natives, sons of the land and the sons of our noblemen and vassals and our relatives, because the thieves and men of bad conscience grab them wishing to have the things and wares of this Kingdom which they are ambitious of, they grab them and get them to be sold; and so great, Sir, is the corruption and licentiousness that our country is being completely depopulated . . . Moreover, Sir, in our Kingdoms there is another great inconvenience which is of little service to God, and this is that many of our people, keenly desirous as they are of the wares and things of your Kingdoms, which are brought here by your people, and in order to satisfy their voracious appetite, seize many of our people, freed and exempt men, and very often it happens that they kidnap even noblemen and the sons of noblemen, and our relatives, and take them to be sold to the white men who are in our Kingdoms; and for this purpose they have concealed them; and others are brought during the night so that they might not be recognized.

And as soon as they are taken by the white men they are immediately ironed and branded with fire, and when they are carried to be embarked, if they are caught by our guards' men the whites allege that they have bought them but they cannot say from whom, so that it is our duty to do justice and to restore to the freemen their freedom, but it cannot be done if your subjects feel offended, as they claim to be.

Notice that King Afonso did not question the practice of slavery per se; it was a long established custom and perfectly legal in Africa as well as the rest of the world. What was Afonso worried about? Why was Afonso having trouble restraining the illegal slave trade? What did he think was causing it? Write a letter back as though you are King João. Remember that João has to balance his need for his African trade with his conscience and also remember that the Africans are militarily superior in their own country to the Portuguese. How would you solve the problem? How could you adjust the economic demands so that the slave trade becomes less lucrative?

☺ ☺ ☺ **EXPLORATION: Triangular Trade Map**

Triangular trade occurs when a place to which goods are imported have no goods required in the original port. For example, African slaves were traded to Caribbean and North American ports in exchange for raw goods which were taken to Europe where they were turned into manufactured goods and traded in Africa for African slaves. Since New England was a vital part of the slave trade triangle, they didn't want the slave trade to end any more than southern planters did. If it did, who would they sell rum and manufactured items to?

Use the Triangle Trade Map from the end of this unit to show the triangular trade routes. Trace the routes. Label the continents and the Atlantic Ocean. Color the map.

☺ ☺ **EXPLORATION: Conditions Aboard A Slave Ship**

Slaves were stowed below deck on trading ships. On average, slaves had about 6 square feet of deck space each, which isn't much if you want to lay down. There wasn't much fresh air and life below deck could feel suffocating. Often they were chained, cuffed, or shackled. They had a very limited diet too – mostly beans, rice, and water, and even that wasn't in big enough quantities.

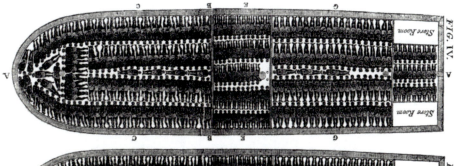

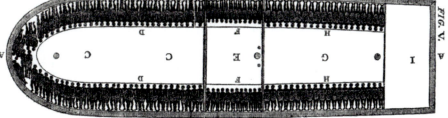

Some slaves aboard the ships were so miserable they tried to kill themselves, either by starving themselves or jumping from the ship to drown in the Atlantic Ocean. Some slaves actually tried to join together and revolt aboard the ships.

Read this firsthand account of a slave ship by a man who was part of a crew whose job it was to apprehend slave ships and return

On The Web

This is an interactive map from the BBC about the slave trade and its abolition. http://www.bbc.co.uk/history/british/abolition/launch_anim_slavery.shtml

We especially like the narrative of Equiano's life. Read it with your kids.

On the Web

If you want firsthand accounts and details of the slave trade visit http://www.slavevoyages.org/tast/index.faces. If you have ancestors who were slaves you might even be able to find information about them on this site.

Additional Layer

Oddly, to our modern sensibilities, the abolitionists and freed slaves had to try to prove that Africans were actually humans, fully equal before God and the law, to other races, as seen by much of the literature and propaganda of the time.

Are there any groups of people today in various countries who are seen as sub-human and therefore without rights?

Additional Layer

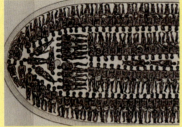

Portuguese slave ships were notorious for the numbers of slaves lost due to abhorrent conditions aboard ships. For example, in one trip a ship lost over 120 slaves who suffocated in the holds. The sailors refused to open the ports because they were afraid of a rebellion. This tragedy led to the crown passing more laws on the slave trade, including the Law of 1684 which required passengers to receive a set amount of water every day and three meals daily. Even with more legislation, life was awful aboard the ships.

Additional Layer

This medallion is the symbol of the British Anti-slavery Society.

the slaves to their homes in Africa:
http://www.eyewitnesstohistory.com/slaveship.htm

Historians estimate that perhaps 2 million slaves died of abuse, harsh conditions, starvation, suffocation, and disease while being transported across the Atlantic. Design a memorial for the victims of the slave trade. You can look up memorials for the Holocaust, 9-11, and others online for inspiration and to see how memorials are constructed. Keep in mind that the purpose of a memorial is to honor the dead as well as to remind us of the terrible consequences of evil. The memorial should in some way convey the human toll and tragedy of the Middle Passage.

☻ **EXPLORATION: William Wilberforce**
William Wilberforce was a member of parliament in England and, for more than 20 years, tried to get slavery, and in particular the slave trade, outlawed in England and in all English holdings.

Until Wilberforce, very few questioned the morality of slavery. Americans had begun questioning slavery during the time of the founders, but there was not enough sympathy or understanding among the majority of the people to outlaw slavery, though they did manage to stop the importation of new slaves from Africa.

Watch this short introduction about William Wilberforce:
https://youtu.be/9dRRpjYg7R0

Then read his famous 1789 speech before the House of Commons:
http://www.bartleby.com/268/4/8.html

Now discuss the speech. Here are questions to get started with:

1. Name one of Wilberforce's arguments against the slave trade. Do you agree with his argument? What opposite argument was he refuting? (repeat with other arguments)
2. When reading the speech, could you imagine and sympathize with the conditions of the Middle Passage? What words did Wilberforce use to make this seem so vivid?
3. How did people arguing in favor of the way slaves were treated in the Middle Passage justify and formulate language to make the Middle Passage seem benign?
4. Wilberforce entered into a twenty year long fight for a cause that had almost no sympathy when he began. He had no idea if he would ever make a difference, but he knew he had to try. Are there any modern day causes you think are worth the kind of sacrifice and effort that Wilberforce put into the cause that was close to his heart?

☻ ☻ EXPLORATION : The Slavery Debate

Hold a mock debate based on the arguments for and against the slave trade of the day. Provide kids with some of these basic arguments and let them fill in their own details. Prepare questions to help keep the debate going and then serve as the moderator. Here are the main bullet points of each side of the debate:

Pro-Slavery Lobby:
- Slave trade was necessary to the success and wealth of Britain.
- If Britain did not engage in the trade then others would. If Britain ceased to trade in slaves with Africa, their commercial rivals, the French and the Dutch, would soon fill the gap and the Africans would be in a much worse situation.
- Africa was already involved in slavery. They had been enslaving each other for years. Being sold to the Americas could actually save their lives.
- Taking Africans from their homeland actually benefited them because they would have more advantages than in Africa.
- The enslaved people were unfit for other work.
- The enslaved people were not ill-treated unless rebellious.
- Slavery was accepted in the Bible.

Anti-Slavery Lobby:
- There were alternatives to the trade; seeds, minerals, crafts, and other goods could be used to fill trade ships.
- If something is wrong, it is wrong whether others do it or not. Just because others are doing it, it doesn't make it right.
- The slavery that existed in Africa was very different from the Transatlantic Slave Trade. The slave trade encouraged African wars and raids to capture slaves.
- The African people were in no way inferior, but equal.
- The trade was damaging to African civilization.
- The Africans suffered greatly from being removed from their homeland. Conditions on the ships were terrible. They had a terribly low life expectancy on the plantations, and many would have preferred death to being enslaved.
- It was morally wrong and, as a Christian country, Britain should not be involved.

☻ ☻ EXPLORATION: The Middle Passage

Have your kids pack into a tight space – under a table, on a couch, or inside an empty bathtub. You can fill in with stuffed animals if you need more bodies. Once they are as tightly packed as possible (without anyone actually getting hurt) ask them how

Famous Folks

The Quaker teacher, Anthony Benezet, was always horrified at the suggestion that the Africans were in any way inferior. He claimed his experiences, gained during 20 years teaching black pupils, proved this was not the case.

Additional Layer
We highly recommend watching "Amazing Grace" with your teens during this unit. The movie is about William Wilberforce and the fight to end the slave trade.

Additional Layer
The song "Amazing Grace" was written by John Newton, a man who spent years as a slave trader. He was caught in a storm and, fearing for his life, promised God that if he were spared he would repent and devote his life to God. He lived to write the hymn. Listen to the words: https://youtu.be/DDDlxmsciqY

Additional Layer

Very few slaves came directly from Africa to the American Colonies. Those who were imported came from the Caribbean, but American slavery was mostly self sustaining with the births of black children.

Teaching Tip

Each day that you're working on a unit, spend a minute or two reviewing what you've already learned. By the end of the two weeks you will have reviewed the information many times. Repetition is the best way to retain knowledge, so go over the same things again and again. Turn it into a game for points or a small prize.

Additional Layer

In 1820 the *Antelope*, a Spanish slaver, was captured by a U.S. privateer off the coast of Florida. The U.S. and Britain had made slave trading illegal, informing foreign governments that any slavers taken on the high seas would be treated as pirates. The *Antelope* Case made it to the Supreme Court of the United States. Most of the slaves aboard were eventually transported as free men to Liberia. Learn more.

they feel. Now ask them how they would like to spend the next five or six weeks in that space. Explain that this is how tightly slaves brought from Africa were packed into slave ships, except they were chained under the decks of a ship without light or air. They had to lie there in their own urine, feces, and vomit. They got very little to eat or drink and most of them got sick during the voyage. This trip was known as the Middle Passage. Almost half of all slaves died during or just after their trip of the Middle Passage.

Read this firsthand account by Equiano, a boy who was kidnapped at the age of 10 and brought to the New World as a slave. He later worked with William Wilberforce to end slavery: http://discoveringbristol.org.uk/slavery/routes/from-africa-to-america/ship-journals/enslaved-african-account/.

😊 🙂 EXPLORATION: The End of the Slave Trade

William Wilberforce was a British member of parliament who could see how evil slavery was. He fought for twenty years to get it abolished by England. At the end of this unit you will find a printable paper craft about William Wilberforce. Print it on to card stock or heavy paper. Color Wilberforce, then cut out the pieces. Write quotes from Wilberforce in the spaces. Fold and glue the long rectangle into a box. Attach the arms. Then make two small paper chains (we wrote words about the evils of slavery on our links) and glue each half into Wilberforce's hands showing how he broke the chains of slavery for the whole world.

GEOGRAPHY: BRAZIL

Brazil was a colony of Portugal from 1500 until 1815 when it became a Portuguese kingdom. In 1822 Brazil achieved complete independence from Portugal and instituted a constitutional monarchy with a parliament. In 1889 a military coup proclaimed a republic. Since then Brazil has been politically stable.

The Pantanal is the largest swamp in the world.

The largest country in South America, Brazil borders every South American country except Chile and Ecuador. The far northern part of Brazil is in the hilly Guiana highlands, then descends into the Amazon Basin, a vast tropical rainforest, parts of which have still never been explored. Further to the south there are more hills and mountains in the Brazilian highlands. The climate is hot, tropical, and wet, with little variation throughout the year. In the far south there are temperate cool winters with occasional frosts.

Brazilian exports include aircraft, textiles and clothing, iron ore, steel, coffee, orange juice, and other agricultural and technology products. Oil reserves have recently been discovered in Brazil, and the industry is just beginning to boom. The economy is mixed between socialism and capitalism, with basically free markets coupled with government oversight, regulation, and taxation of business.

Additional Layer

The name "Brazil" comes from the Brazilwood tree. There were once many of these trees along Brazil's coast, but the trees were harvested for their dark red dye, greatly reducing their number.

On The Web

Homeschool Share has a free printable lapbook about Brazil that would be a great companion to this unit:

http://www.homeschool share.com/country_bra zil.php

On the Web

This is a 59 minute video on Brazil from the BBC: https://youtu.be/7ejbwD jp9aw

Fabulous Facts

Brazil is the fifth largest country in the world in terms of land area. It has varied natural resources and a huge amount of biodiversity.

Famous Folks

Carmen Miranda was a dancer and actress from Brazil who made it big in Hollywood. She is iconic for her role in *The Gang's All Here* in which she wore a hat decorated with fruit. She now has her image on every bunch of Chiquita bananas you buy.

On The Web

Check out http://youtu.be/NDphdusk_jg to get a taste for what Brazilian Carnaval is like from the costumes and music to the huge crowds. It isn't in English, but you can see the visually stunning show nonetheless. It's pretty long, but you can just skim through and watch bits to get a feel for the celebration.

Additional Layer

You can review rhythm with your maracas.

☺ ☺ ☺ EXPLORATION: Map of Brazil

Use the map from the end of this unit. Label it and color it.

Places to label:
- Atlantic Ocean
- Amazon River
- Rio Negro
- Rio Tocantins
- Rio Tapajos
- Rio Sao Francisco
- Brasilia
- Goiania
- Porto Alegre
- Curitiba
- Sao Paulo
- Campinas
- Rio de Janeiro
- Salvador
- Recife
- Fortaleza
- Belem
- Manaus

☺ ☺ EXPLORATION: Paper Maracas

Make a paper plate maraca. First, paint or color the back of a paper plate in a Brazilian theme: flag of Brazil, Brazilian animal, Brazil soccer team colors, etc.

Once the paint is dry, fold the plate in half and staple the rounded side most of the way closed. Then pour dry pasta or beans into the plate. Staple it closed the rest of the way. Shake your maraca to make music.

Garrett and Harrison are holding the paper plate maracas they made (we used dessert-sized plates). CJ is wearing a Carnaval mask (see the following directions).

☺ ☻ EXPLORATION: Carnaval

Carnaval, known as Mardi Gras in the United States, is a celebration in many Catholic countries just before Lent, a time of restraint and sacrifice. In Brazil people march through the streets in parades, wearing fabulous masks and costumes. The Carnaval parade in Rio de Janeiro is the largest in the world and is very famous for its opulence.

Make a Carnaval mask from thin cardboard or poster board. Cut out the mask shape you desire and decorate it with paint, glitter, feathers, beads, and so on. Tape a craft stick or a straw to the bottom as a handle to hold the mask up to your face.

☺ ☻ ☻ EXPLORATION: Amazon Rainforest

The Amazon Rainforest is the largest rainforest in the world. Over half of it is found in Brazil. There are over 40,000 different kinds of plants there, and the layers within the rainforest support different kinds of plants and animals.

Create a mural that shows the different levels within a rainforest. Start with a large sheet of butcher paper and draw the different levels of the rainforest:

- The emergent layer is at the top. There are large trees that poke up out of the canopy that make up this layer. Sloths, spider monkeys, macaws, hummingbirds, harpy eagles, goliath bird-eating tarantuals, butterflies, bats, snakes, and insects live in the emergent layer. Animals this high must be lightweight and comfortable with life in the trees and sunshine.

Additional Layer

Most rainforests are found right around the equator. This is because equatorial lands are suitably warm and wet for their growth.

Even though they are mostly found in those limited areas, they are a benefit to the entire planet because they produce a huge amount of oxygen through photosynthesis. They are sometimes called "the lungs of the earth." They also support a huge number of plant and animal species that aren't found anywhere else on the earth.

Additional Layer

Cocoa is one of the leading exports of Brazil. Find out where cocoa comes from.

Additional Layer

The Amazon Rainforest is being cleared for farm land, mostly cattle grazing and soybean production. Some people are concerned that clearing too much forest will destroy irreplaceable species, change the climate of Brazil and other tropical countries, and lead to a less healthy planet overall. Find out more about this issue and what the problems are.

Additional Layer

The canopy is made up of an interlocking network of sun-hungry leaves. It is super efficient! Only 3 to 15 percent of sunlight penetrates the canopy to reach the lower under-growth.

Photo by Ben Sutherland, CC license, Wikimedia.

Not all of the light is caught by the topmost leaves. Leaves at the top of the canopy are angled so they aren't fully ex-posed to the sun. If they weren't they would get burned from the intense heat. That also allows more sunlight to filter through to the leaves that are lower.

Leaves lower down, un-like those at the top of the canopy, grow hori-zontally to capture all the rays reaching them. The leaves actually move and change angles depending on the amount of sun-light they need. The leaf angles also change to ac-count for wet, cloudy seasons and dry, sunny seasons. The plants adapt to meet their needs.

- The canopy is a thick layer of trees. The top of the canopy is exposed to sunlight, but the thick trees make shade beneath it. Animals like howler monkeys, sakis, insects, pygmy anteaters, macaws, and poison-arrow frogs live in the canopy.
- The understory is below the canopy. It is a shady, moist place where lots of ferns and mosses and fungi grow. Jaguars, leopards, and possums all jump into the trees for rest. They spend their time between the understory and the forest floor.
- The rainforest floor is the layer of decomposing leaves and wood that makes rich soil. The forest floor is home to tapirs, bush dogs, jungle cats, white tailed deer, goutis, and many venomous reptiles.

Label each part once you've drawn it and include caption boxes to describe the layers of the rainforest. Choose some rainforest plants and animals to read about, then add pictures of those species with caption boxes on your mural as well.

😊 😊 😊 EXPLORATION: Rainforest Animals

Rainforests are one of the most diverse plant and animal ecosystems. They provide homes for a huge number of plant and animal species. The Amazon Rainforest is the home to about 10% of the world's known animal species and 20% of the world's bird species. Not all the animals there are so friendly; there are many predators like cougars, jaguars, and anacondas. Go to www.tropical-rainforest-animals.com and choose a species of animal to write an animal report on. Make sure to add your animal to your rainforest mural.

☺ ☺ ☺ EXPLORATION: Samba Music

Samba music is endemic to Brazil and is a mixture of the Portuguese and African heritage of the country. It uses a fast, heavy beat and various percussion instruments such as tambourines, maracas, and drums, plus guitars and keyboards. Samba dance includes lots of fancy footwork and hip movements. It is fun to watch.

Get some samba music from the library to listen to or look for a You Tube video of Samba music with dance – *cough* you'll want to preview before you show your kids, most of the costumes are skimpy. There are a few videos that show you some basic Samba dance steps too.

Here is a tasteful one that shows very basic steps:
http://youtu.be/91G3MqgOcbM

☺ ☺ EXPLORATION: Flag of Brazil

The Flag of Brazil is called the Auriverde (means gold and green). The gold represents the minerals of Brazil and the green represents the forests. The blue globe in the center shows a night sky with 27 stars, each one representing a state in the country. The 27 stars are arranged to pattern the night sky on November

15th, 1889, the day that Brazil was made a republic. The band across the globe says "Ordem e Progresso" which means "Order and Progress."

Use the flag coloring sheet from the end of the unit to color as you talk about the meaning of Brazil's flag.

☺ EXPLORATION: Land of The Parrots

When sailors and explorers encountered Brazil's coastline they called it the Land of the Parrots. There are about 30 different species of parrots in the Amazon Rainforest. Several known species have become extinct already. Parrots are very brightly colored birds. They are known for their curved beaks and are thought to be very intelligent. Most parrots live in tropical areas of the world.

Choose a species of Amazon parrot to read about. Then make this parrot craft with a colorful tissue paper tail. Just draw a simple parrot outline, cut out a yellow beak and feet, and then glue small squares of tissue paper on to your parrot's tail. You can look at a

Additional Layer

Samba music is the most well known Brazilian music outside of Brazil, but the country has pioneered dozens of different styles. Two popular ones are Choro and Bossa Nova.

This is Joaquim Callado, one developers of Choro music.

Famous Folks

Pedro Cabral was a Spanish explorer and the discoverer of Brazil.

Cabral and his men sighting the Brazilian coast in 1500.

Fabulous Fact

Brazil has been a Catholic country from its founding by the Portuguese. But the many native religions, as well as African religions imported with slaves, have melded with the Catholic faith.

Additional Layer

Iguazu Falls is a huge series of waterfalls along the Iguazu River. There are many islands and around 275 different falls. The series of waterfalls is huge and impressive. When she saw it, Eleanor Roosevelt was reported to say, "Poor Niagara!"

Photo shared by gicar93

Fabulous Fact

Capoeira is a Brazilian martial art sometimes played as a game. Learn more.

Fabulous Fact

Soccer is Brazil's second religion. Brazil is the only country that has played in every world cup.

This is Brazil vs. Cameroon, Brazil in yellow jerseys, during the 2014 World Cup. Photo by copa2014.gov.br , CC license, Wikimedia.

picture of your species of parrot and create the same colorful feathers that it has. You can also color your parrot's body in and color the background of your page if you'd like to.

EXPLORATION: Brazilian Black Beans

Beans and rice are a Brazilian staple, and there are countless recipes and ways to make them. Here's a simple preparation.

3 cans black beans, drained
½ Tbsp. vegetable oil
4 pieces bacon, diced
1 yellow onion, diced
1 clove garlic, minced

½ tsp. ground cumin
salt
red pepper flakes
ground black pepper
fresh cilantro

1. Heat the oil in a small frying pan. Saute bacon pieces in oil for about 3 minutes, stirring occasionally. Add onion and saute more until the onions and bacon are dark brown.
2. Add garlic, cumin, salt, pepper, and red pepper flakes. Stir.
3. Add beans, mix it all well, and allow it to simmer for about 20 minutes, uncovered.
4. Remove about a cup of the beans and smash them into a paste. Return the paste to the rest of the bean mixture and stir. Season with more salt, pepper, and cilantro to taste.
5. Serve over white rice and the meat of your choice. Pulled pork is delicious with this.

Brazilian Black Beans served over rice with a fried banana and bacon wrapped pork

😊 😊 😊 **EXPLORATION: Kayapo**

There are hundreds of native tribes in Brazil. One of these is the Kayapo. Their story is fairly typical in Brazil. The Kayapo lived by farming small plots of ground, cleared in the forest by slash and burn techniques, for six or seven years until the soil was depleted. Then they moved on, allowing the forest to regrow in the vacant fields. Their way of life had little impact on the forest health as a whole, but required a lot of land. Then the Brazilians came along and wanted to mine and log the forest lands of the Kayapo. They took by force what they could not take by law. Eventually the Kayapo reached an agreement that the miners could use some of the lands in return for a percentage of the profits. The money helped the Kayapo build better houses and secure educations for their children, but the mining poisoned the water with mercury, harming the health of the animals and the people. The struggles between the Kayapo and the industrialists and ranchers have often turned bloody. Today some of the lands of the Kayapo are protected by the government, but there are frequent violations, including those by the government itself, and violence is still always on the horizon.

Watch this video from Khan Academy about the Kayapo people and their headdresses. https://youtu.be/irYfbY_jryY.

Additional Layer

The official and universal language of Brazil is Portuguese. It is the only country in the western hemisphere which speaks Portuguese, and that sets Brazil apart from the rest of Central and South America.

You can check out some Portuguese vocabulary and even learn the language at www.duolingo.com, a free language learning site.

Fabulous Fact

This is the *Christ The Redeemer* statue in Rio de Janiero, Brazil. The statue is 98 feet tall and sits at the peak of a mountain overlooking the city. It was built between 1922 and 1931 by artist Paul Landowski and engineer Heitor da Silva Costa.

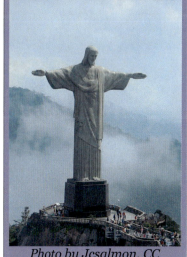

Photo by Jcsalmon, CC license, Wikimedia

Additional Layer

Brazilians, especially the upper classes in the big cities, are obsessed with physical appearance. Anyone with the money to do so enhances their bodies and makes themselves beautiful. In fact, if you want to climb into a higher social strata you must appear beautiful. Beauty to a Brazilian is a thin frame, light colored skin, and European features. A common sentiment in Brazil is that "there are no ugly people, only poor people." Brazilians spend more money on cosmetics, clothes, and plastic surgery per capita than any other place on earth. Think about the implications of their priorities and values. Do you agree or disagree?

Additional Layer

Tiradentes Day in Brazil celebrates the man who was killed after he led a movement to overthrow the colonial government.

Tiradentes Day is mostly honored by Brazilians today by taking a day off of work and school. Few remember the significance or the sacrifice of their founder.

Are there holidays that your country has forgotten the meaning of?

☺ ☺ ☺ EXPLORATION: Bumba Meu Boi

Bumba Meu Boi is a traditional folk tale told in Brazil. Every Brazilian knows the story. It is played out in the street during the Festival of the Ox, in June or at Christmas time, depending on the region. The story goes that a pregnant woman has an insatiable craving for ox tongue and convinces her husband to get her some. He kills an ox, which belongs to his master. The master is furious and pursues the poor husband all over the countryside, finally capturing him and sentencing him to death. But the ox is magically restored to life and the owner of the ox must pardon the man to the rejoicing of all the people.

Here is a short clip showing some actors and musicians in the street acting out the story. The bull is wildly colorful.
https://youtu.be/Rpy7ovT-dYo

Make a bull costume with a cardboard box, paint, and construction paper. First, paint the box a bright color all over. Then let the kids decorate with paint any way they like. Once it dries, add a cut out of an ox head to the front of the box. Finish it off by adding a fringe of colorful construction paper around the bottom edge of the whole box. Just cut the construction paper into thin strips, leaving one edge attached to make fringe.

SCIENCE: MINERALS & GEMS

A mineral is a solid, naturally occurring chemical substance with a specific chemical composition. They are not alive and never have been. Some are very common, like silver, quartz, halite, and copper, while others are very rare. Some minerals are made of a single type of element, others are salts, and some are much more complex. They are all made up of a chemical mixture of elements from the periodic table, and so they all have chemical formulas.

Here are a few examples:

Quartz: SiO_2

Alkali Feldspar: $(K,Na)AlSi_3O_8$

Biotite: $K(Fe,Mg)_3AlSi_3O_{10}(OH)_2$

Halite: $NaCl$

Calcite is made of calcium, carbon, and oxygen ($CaCO3$)

Rocks are made up of minerals. Often one rock will have several kinds of minerals within it. That means that all the rocks you see around you – the mountains, the canyons, riverbeds, and the entire crust of the earth – are made up of minerals that have joined together, forming rocks. Scientists examine the minerals to learn how the rock was formed.

Some common gemstones

A gem is a mineral you can cut and polish and wear as jewelry. They aren't chemically different; we just call them gemstones because we prize them for their beauty. Because precious gems are rare they are more valuable. Semi-precious gems are more common and less valuable, though more valuable than a common rock.

Fabulous Fact

There are about 4,000 known minerals, but only a dozen or so are common in the earth's crust.

Additional Layer

There are three categories of inorganic solids: crystals, poly-crystals (many small crystals joined together into one solid mass), and amorphous (no crystals). Find some solid matter in your house and decide which category it fits into.

Crystals: salt grains, diamond ring, snowflake

Poly-crystals: metal, ice cube, ceramics, rocks

Amorphous: plastics, wax, glass

Fabulous Fact

Crystals with flat faces (sides) are called euhedral. Crystals without flat faces are called anhedral. Anhedral crystals are generally one grain within a poly-crystal. Euhedral crystals have regular plane angles which reveal the atomic structure that makes up the larger crystal. You can identify a crystal by the angle of its faces.

The Properties of Minerals

The properties of minerals help us identify them. Here are the basic things geologists look at:

- luster
- cleavage
- streak
- specific gravity
- hardness

You can see that the mineral tests from the explorations are really just looking at the properties of minerals.

Fabulous Fact

Some living things can produce crystals with their bodies. Pearls are poly-crystals formed by mollusks.

Photo by Mauro Cateb, CC license, Wikimedia.

Fabulous Fact

Hardness can be compared to household items like glass and a nail, but it can also be observed by comparing minerals with other minerals. Mohs Hardness Scale is a continuum of minerals arranged by their hardness.

☺ ☺ ☺ EXPLORATION: Mineral Cookies

Get out some cookie ingredients and set them on the counter in bowls:

flour	sugar
eggs	baking powder
butter	chocolate chips
raisins	peanut butter
oatmeal	mini chocolate chips

The ingredients you placed out are like minerals in rocks. Using the same minerals combined in different amounts and under different temperatures and conditions makes different rocks. If you combine the cookie ingredients in different ways you'll get all different cookies.

Have each child make up their own cookies using the ingredients. Don't give them a recipe, just allow them to experiment. Bake the cookies and then taste them to see how using the same basic ingredients you can get such a variety of cookies. It's the same way with rocks.

☺ ☺ EXPERIMENT: Mohs Scale

For this experiment you need samples of minerals. You can get a set of Mohs minerals at Home Science Tools. Label the samples with letters A through I using sticky dots.

Minerals can be classified and identified by how hard they are. If a mineral can scratch another mineral then it is harder than the one it scratches. Minerals are placed along a scale of hardness from 1 to 10. The scale is called Mohs scale.

This is a box of ten minerals, each of which corresponds to a number on the Mohs hardness scale. Image by Hannes Grobe, CC license, Wikimedia.

At the end of this unit you will find a lab sheet with the Mohs mineral scale on it. Using a sample of minerals, see if you can put your minerals in order from softest to hardest. Write the letter of your labeled mineral on the lab sheet.

☺ ☻ EXPERIMENT: Mineral Tests

Geologists test minerals for hardness, reactivity, magnetism, streak color and specific gravity in order to identify them. Here you'll learn how to do all of these tests. Coupled with the mineral identification flowchart from the printables section of this unit, you can identify the minerals in your collection. You can buy a collection of minerals to test from Home Science Tools for about $15. (They have several very cool rock, gem, and mineral kits; check them out and pick your favorite.)

Hardness: Rocks are categorized according to how hard they are on a scale of 1 to 10. The softest rocks are a 1 (talc) the hardest rocks are a 10 (diamond).

1	2	3	4	5	6	7	8	9
TALC very soft, like chalk	GYPSUM easily scratched with a nail	CALCITE difficult to scratch with a nail	FLUORITE cannot be scratch with a nail	APATITE about the hardness of teeth	MICRO-CLINE suitable for gems	QUARTZ scratches glass	TOPAZ harder than quartz	RUBY harder than to-paz	DIAMOND hardest material known to man

Compare the hardness of a rock to various common items to estimate where they are on the hardness scale. If the item can scratch the rock, it's harder; if it cannot, then the rock is softer.

Fingernail	2.5		Glass	5.5
Copper	3.5		Iron Nail	6.5

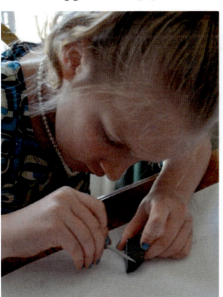
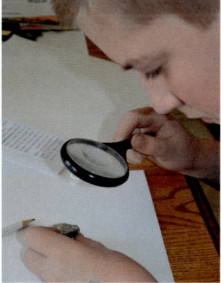

Fabulous Fact

Some groups of atoms can form more than one type, or allotrope, of crystals. Graphite and diamond are both allotropes of pure carbon. They have identical atomic formulas, but their crystal structure differs. The same is true of SiO_2, it can form glass or quartz crystals.

Fabulous Fact

Pencils have a mineral called graphite in them. Every time you write with a pencil you are dong a streak test!

Additional Layer

The more time a crystal has to form, the larger it will become. Crystals that form slowly and deep within the earth can become quite large. In contrast, when lava spews from the earth and the rock cools quickly, there isn't enough time for large crystals to form. You won't see big crystal formations in obsidian because it cools rapidly.

This is an emerald crystal from a mine in Columbia. Photo by Didier Descouens, CC license, Wikimedia.

Fabulous Fact

Idaho is called the Gem State because the mountains are especially rich with all kinds of rare and valuable minerals and gems.

Streak: Scrape a piece of a mineral across an unglazed piece of white tile. It will leave behind a streak of color. The color of the streak can help you identify which mineral you have. The streak left behind may not be the same as the color you see in the mineral. Use this website to check your streak color against mineral types:
http://webmineral.com/help/Streak.shtml#.VQRQ3o7F8xg

Luster: Look at the sample and decide if it has a metallic or non-metallic look. If it is non-metallic, decide whether it looks shiny and glassy, greasy, waxy, or dull.

Cleavage: Check to see how your mineral breaks. A mineral with good cleavage breaks along flat planes into sheets, like mica. Poor cleavage means it will split in irregular forms or completely shatter.

Chemical Reaction: Determine if the specimen fizzes, giving off CO_2 when a few drops of a weak acid, like vinegar, is applied. If it does fizz, then your specimen contains calcium carbonate, like calcite and argonite. You can just drop a bit of vinegar on your sample to test for this one.

You'll also look for a few other identifying features, like color and presence of crystals, which can often best be seen using a small hand lens or magnifying glass.

☺ ☻ EXPERIMENT: Borax Crystals

Many minerals and gems have a crystalline structure, that is, they form in regular shapes. Salt, for example, always forms in a cube shape. Look at some salt crystals under a magnifying glass or microscope.

You can grow some beautiful borax crystals with borax (found in the laundry aisle), water, and pipe cleaners.

1. Bend a pipe cleaner into the shape you want: a snowflake or star or some other shape.
2. Tie the pipe cleaner to a piece of string and the other end of the string to the center of a pencil or craft stick.

3. Combine 1 cup of boiling water with Borax, 1 tablespoonful at a time until you can stir no more Borax in the water (this is a saturated solution, meaning it can't hold any more solute).
4. Add food coloring in your favorite color to the water.
5. Pour the solution into a clear jar and place your pipe cleaner into the solution, suspended from the string and the pencil above.
6. Let it sit overnight and then come and check out your crystals. What shape did they form in? Look at them under a microscope.

☺ ☻ ☻ EXPERIMENT: Salt and Vinegar Crystals

Many crystals are formed from ionically attracted elements, also known as salts. Salts are formed with ionic bonds, or connections between elements. An ionic bond is formed from elements that are undergoing attraction based on charges. We can make large colorful salt and vinegar crystals overnight.

To grow your own you'll need:

- vinegar
- food coloring
- salt
- hot water
- a sponge
- a shallow dish

The procedure:
1. Cut up a sponge and place pieces into the bottom of your shallow dish. You can do as many or as few sponge pieces as you like. We used three irregularly shaped sponge pieces from a previous project.
2. Bring some water to a boil.

Additional Layer

Not all crystals are salts. Think of sugar crystals. Sugar is made from long carbon chains, which are formed with covalent bonds, not salty at all. Protein can also form crystals in zero gravity as NASA scientists have proved.

This photo is a collage of different crystals grown on the International Space Station or MIR from different proteins that can be found in living things.

On the Web

Watch this 5 minute clip on a fantastic crystal cave in Mexico.
https://youtu.be/wgUFb_l4DLE

3. Mix 1 cup of the boiling water with 1/4 cup salt and 1 Tbsp. of vinegar. Stir the salt in, and dissolve as much as you can.
4. Pour the hot salt water over your sponges in the dish and allow the sponges to absorb the water for a moment.
5. Put one drop of food coloring on each piece of sponge. You can use all the same color or chose several different colors.
6. Let the salt water sit overnight.
7. Check on your salt crystals to see how they are doing. If you let it sit for longer, even more crystals will grow.

In the case of the salt and vinegar crystals, you are really just growing table salt crystals. Table salt is made of sodium (Na) and chlorine (Cl), so the formula for table salt is NaCl. The sodium (Na) is in the first column of the Periodic Table. All elements in the first column of the table have one electron they would very much like to get rid of; these elements are very reactive. Chlorine (Cl) is in the second to last column of the periodic table. It has seven electrons orbiting in the outermost level of electrons. More than anything in the world chlorine wants to have eight electrons. It is also very reactive. Oh, look! Sodium has one electron it would like to give up and chlorine really wants one more. They react!

But when you made your crystals, you didn't see any reaction at all. Why not? Because the sodium and chlorine were never decomposed (separated), they were just dissolved. Dissolving means that large crystals break down into individual atoms interspersed with the atoms of the liquid they are dissolved in. The dissolved atoms are too small to see, so it looks like they just disappear, but they're there waiting to come out of solution. That is what happens when you make crystals, the liquid dries up, leaving behind large crystals of salt.

☺ ☺ ☺ EXPERIMENT: Make a Geode

A geode is a plain looking rock that is hollow on the inside and has a crystal filled cavity. You can make a model geode with alum (find it in the spice aisle), an egg shell, and some food coloring.

1. Prepare some egg shell halves by washing them out and drying them. Paint the egg shells with a thin coating of glue, attach some of the undissolved alum to the insides of the egg shell and allow to dry.
2. Boil water and measure out a ¼ cup.

3. Add alum to the water, 1 teaspoonful at a time, until you can stir no more in, making a saturated solution.
4. Set your egg shell half into a small dish, just large enough to hold it. Then pour the saturated solution over the egg shell until it is completely submerged.
5. Let it sit overnight or for a couple of days until your crystals grow.

☺ ☺ ☺ EXPLORATION: Mmmm, Mmmm Minerals
Your body needs 60 different minerals in order to be healthy. You don't need to eat dirt and rocks to get them though. Much of the healthy food we eat is grown in mineral-rich soil. Animals we eat have also eaten plants and so have minerals within them too. Take a trip to the grocery store and go on a mineral scavenger hunt. There's a printable scavenger hunt at the end of this unit.

☺ ☺ ☺ EXPLORATION: Gems

Gemstones are made from especially hard crystals. Generally speaking, the harder and more clear the gem, the more valuable it will be. They are valuable because they are rare, much harder to find than more common minerals.

Gems are usually formed deeper within the earth than other minerals, so often we must dig, or mine, for them. Once they are dug out and separated from the

---

Additional Layer

Amethyst, a purple variety of quartz, was a precious and rare gem for thousands of years, but then in 1902 huge quantities of amethysts were found in Brazilian mines and the gems dropped in value. Today they are considered semi-precious. Think about how supply affects the value we place on things. The whole history of amethysts is fascinating. Look it up and learn more.

Additional Layer

Every month has a birthstone. What is your birthstone?

Fabulous Fact

Natural gemstones are rare, but people have learned to manufacture artificial gemstones in laboratories and factories. Diamonds, emeralds, and rubies, have all been produced in labs and made into jewelry. Lab produced gems have all the same characteristics and atomic structure as natural gems, except without the impurities and irregularities that can occur in natural gems. Natural gems are still more highly priced and prized though.

rock around them, they are then polished and cut. They are cut in special ways to make them shine and reflect the most light. Before they are cut they look like colorful rocks.

Go visit http://www.minerals.net/GemStoneMain.aspx. Choose one of the gemstones to read about. Draw a picture of your gem and write interesting tidbits about it on the page. Then share the information you've found in an oral report while showing your illustration.

☺ ☺ ☺ EXPLORATION: Carats

Diamonds and other gemstones are weighed in carats. There are five carats in one gram. Originally gems were measured against carob seeds, which were thought to all have the same mass. In truth, the seeds can be quite different, but they were used by merchants nonetheless. The greater the mass, the more carats a gem has. Go visit a jeweler to see the difference in carat sizes of stones. Then research some of the largest stones ever found. Find how how many carats each of these stones has: the Star of Africa, the Green Dresden, the Tiffany Yellow Diamond, the Black Amsterdam Diamond, the Eugenie Blue Diamond, and the Blue Hope Diamond.

☺ ☺ ☺ EXPEDITION: Rock Hound

In the last three units we've been studying rocks, so you probably already have a collection going. Plan another outing to a new location to find more variety in your rock collection. Identify as many of the rocks as you can and display them nicely in an egg carton. Don't forget to label them with the name of the rock and the location it was found.

THE ARTS: COLONIAL ART

The Colonial Period in America was an interesting time, because in many ways the people were thrown back artistically and technologically as they settled in a new land. Very quickly they caught back up with Europe, but there was a period of time when survival was more important than beauty. Art flourishes when there is enough food and industry to allow for plenty of leisure time, but colonial America didn't allow for a lot of leisure. Still, there was art produced. Much of it was furniture and other useful items that the colonists needed.

A recreated workshop in Colonial Williamsburg, Virginia, shared under CC license by Fletcher6

European settlers in America often came with very little. They brought personal belongings, but there were no moving trucks full of household items. The colonists built their own furniture and many of their household items.

☺ ☻ EXPLORATION: Furniture
There were two kinds of furniture being produced in colonial America. The first, called Seventeenth Century, was sturdy and made of mostly right angles and straight pieces. It focused on strong horizontal lines and low seats. Later the style became more sleek, narrow, and curving and was called Baroque. Baroque furniture was more decorative and included scrolls, colored woods, metal inlays, and other flourishes. Vertical lines became the focus. Furniture from this period felt lighter and more ornate.

Fabulous Fact

There were hundreds of semi-trained artists who made their living painting signs, furniture, and portraits. The portrait painters were known as limners. This is a painting of a baby done by an anonymous limner.

Additional Layer

The Baroque style was also known as William and Mary style furniture. It got this name from William III and Mary II, monarchs of England who ruled from 1689 to 1702. The monarchs brought many Dutch and French artisans with them who brought more flourish and decoration to the previously plainer styles.

Go visit the Met Museum's website and click through the slide show of furniture from this period. Try to identify which of these two styles each piece is.

http://www.metmuseum.org/toah/hd/will/hd_will.htm

☺ ☻ ☺ EXPLORATION: Preserving History

One of the unique impacts of art is its ability to preserve history. The colonists didn't have much time or means for the creation of art, but they were certainly busy laying the foundation for a country which went on to be hugely important in the world. Some of the art that was produced told these great true stories.

This bust of George Washington was one of the few sculptures created in America during this period. It was made by William Rush.

Think of this period of time. We are now in a new age with plenty of affluence, time, and technology for creating art. Imagine that you were asked to create one piece of art for a time capsule that would represent your time and your generation. Create a design and make your piece. Make sure that it tells the story of this time in history.

☺ ☻ ☺ EXPLORATION: Portraits

Not many colonial painters could make a living by painting alone, but some did portraits while also painting signs or other useful items. Portraits were the most important art of the time. Many of the American artists were actually Englishmen who had immigrated, so you can see English style within the portraits. They were often idealized rather than perfectly realistic. The objects shown with a person, right down to their clothes, were representative of their wealth, importance, or position.

Most of the portrait artists of the time are not well-known at all. They painted portraits in their day much like we go to a photographer to have our portraits taken today. We may be happy with and appreciate their work, but we don't give them high honors as artists.

Here is a portrait of a a girl named Miss Frances A. Motley. It is thought to have been painted by John Blunt, a portrait painter. Other than her name, which we know because it is included on the card next to her, we don't know who this little girl was. What can you guess about her from the portrait? The artist would have included the most symbolically important things about her in her portrait.

Writer's Workshop

Find a colonial American portrait online and imagine what the person's life is like. Look at the objects surrounding him or her and write a story based on what you know from clues in the painting and what you know of colonial life.

This is a portrait of Mrs. Robert Rogers painted by Joseph Blackburn in 1761 near Boston. Blackburn was a British born painter who spent his career in the American and Caribbean colonies.

Discuss the portrait. Talk about the little girl as well as the author's use of line, shape, texture, color, and space. Talk about the similarities and differences between painted portraits and photographs.

Make a portrait in your sketchbook of someone in your family. Include special items that represent who the person is, including hobbies, personality, and beliefs.

On the Web

This series of articles and videos from Khan Academy discusses early American art.
https://www.khanacademy.org/humanities/monarchy-enlightenment/english-portraiture/america-ageof-revolution/a/portraits-of-john-and-elizabeth-freake-and-their-baby

Fabulous Fact

This is a famous engraving made by Paul Revere, showing the British firing on the Americans during the Boston Massacre. It was not intended to be historically accurate, but to make a political point.

Additional Layer

The Abby Aldritch Rockefeller Folk Art Museum in Colonial Williamsburg has the largest collection of early American folk art in the United States. The collection includes paintings, toys, textiles, furniture, and more. Visit in person or online: http://emuseum.history.org/

On the Web

Have your teens read this article from the National Gallery of Art: https://www.nga.gov/collection/gallery/amer.shtm

☺ ☺ ☺ EXPLORATION: Paul Revere

Paul Revere was a famous silversmith, but even he couldn't support himself with that alone. He used his smithy talents to do engraving, repair jewelry, and make false teeth for his customers. He eventually began working with other metals too and made things like cannons, dishes, and copper bolts. He was well-known for the beautiful dishes that he engraved and sold in his shop. This was very typical of the American colonial period – the most beautiful things also served a purpose to the colonists.

His metalsmithing wasn't used solely for utilitarian purposes; Revere also used his artistry to make prints from metal for engravings.

Now we use many power tools to shape and engrave metal, but colonial silversmiths like Revere didn't have those. Watch this video to see how colonial silversmiths shaped their metal: http://mrnussbaum.com/13-colonies-silversmith/

Make your own etching with a foil pie pan and a pointed stick. You can use a pencil, a kitchen skewer, a long nail, or something similar. Press with the pointed end to create a design on the foil. Punch two holes near the top rim of the pie plate and thread a ribbon through to hang your project.

☺ ☺ ☺ **EXPLORATION: Folk Art**

Fine art is the work of artists, but folk art is the work of the people. It was not created for museums or galleries. It was created for the colonists' homes. Because they were still very focused on the essentials of life, much of their folk art was created on useful items. For example, they may paint a trunk with beautiful designs or stencil a pattern on a bedpost.

Get a useful wooden item like a simple picture frame, a wooden spoon, a flower pot. a birdhouse, or small chest and decorate it in a style that suits you. Folk art was meant to suit the tastes of the "folks," not the masses, so make it reflective of your own tastes.

☺ ☺ ☺ **EXPLORATION: American Folk Painting**

American folk painting was unique and often brightly colored. We don't know who painted most of it, because like other folk art, it wasn't signed or created with a gallery, church, palace, or museum in mind. Look carefully at this early painting of George and Martha Washington. What do you notice about these elements of art within the painting?

- Line – Does it feel geometric or organic?
- Shape – Identify some basic shapes within it and trace your finger along them.
- Texture – What do you notice about the clothing?
- Color – How is color used to make the painting more interesting? How much of the color is realistic?
- Space – Does this look 3 dimensional? Realistic?

Additional Layer

Stenciling was a common practice during this time. People stenciled designs on their furniture, trunks, or other objects as a decoration. You can purchase simple stencils from a craft store or even cut your own from thick paper to try making stenciled designs.

Famous Folks

Edward Hicks is one of the most prolific folk artists of the 19th century. He painted many scenes of his family's farm.

This one is called "Peacable Kingdom," a theme Hicks painted over 100 times.

Additional Layer

Many modern artists are producing gorgeous folk art for a living. You will probably like the art of Cheryl Bartley, Grandma Moses, and Pristine Cartera-Turkus.

On The Web

This 18 minute video explains early American folk art beautifully.

https://youtu.be/sv_ysp 17DIQ

Additional Layer

This painting of slaves on a South Carolina plantation is unique.

It was done by an amateur, most likely a plantation owner named John Rose, in about 1790. It is unusual because the slaves are depicted without bias, engaged in an activity that, for them, would have been normal and enjoyable and having nothing to do with the work on the plantation. It appears that they are dancing or performing a ceremony of some kind. The instruments in the picture are real west African instruments.

On the Web

The Colonial Williamsburg site has information about trades that existed in the colonies.
http://www.history.org/almanack/life/trades/tradehdr.cfm

Create your own painting in this style. Begin with pencil outline of basic shapes of people. Outline important areas using permanent marker. Go back and fill in sections using tempera paints. Once it's dry, add more details with markers.

☺ ☺ ☺ EXPLORATION: Artisan Jobs

Many everyday jobs in colonial America took a fair amount of artistic skills. Go check out some colonial jobs by exploring the colonial town center on King James Street from this website:
http://mrnussbaum.com/13colonies/13trades/

Once you've perused the website, decide on a job that required artistic skills in some way and create a project to present along with an oral report about the profession. You may want to research your profession more and find out the specifics of what those artisans did.

Milliners, hatters, silversmiths, cobblers, printers, basket makers, cabinetmakers, harness makers – all these and more were considered to be artisans. Without factories and mass production, they crafted each of their goods meticulously by hand. There were even professional button makers who handcrafted buttons from seashells, wood, wax, walnuts, and animal bones. It wasn't long before brass buttons were fashionable. Some button makers even painted tiny paintings on their buttons. We used this idea to paint our own button scenes. You can use real buttons or the button printable from this unit.

A miniature painting on a colonial button

EXPLANATION: The Growth of Art in America
As time went on, art became more and more a part of the Americans' lives. The better they were able to meet their basic needs, the more they could focus on beauty and art. Many American artists went to Europe to study painting and other fine art. Americans didn't seem interested in European art of the time though, which mostly focused on historical paintings. Americans wanted portraits, which were seen as inferior by European artists. Eventually Americans found their own new style and voice in landscape paintings of the beautiful frontier lands of America.

Rags to Riches
Caspar Wistar was born in Germany and scrimped and saved to be able to come to the colonies. He had not a penny to his name by the time he arrived in Pennsylvania, but found work collecting ashes for a soap maker.

Soon he became an apprentice to a buttoner. After learning the trade he opened his own button shop and even bought a furnace that allowed him to make metal buttons.

By the time he died he owned land and several businesses, including the first glass making factory in the colonies. He employed 60 people and lived the American dream before America was even her own country.

Coming up next . . .

Unit 3-15

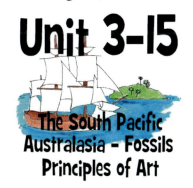

The South Pacific
Australasia - Fossils
Principles of Art

Slavery

Slavery is when one person owns another person, usually forcing them to work for the owner with no payment. Today nearly everyone believes that slavery is wrong, but through most of human history slavery has been normal and accepted. In the late 1700's and 1800's people finally defeated slavery by making it illegal throughout the world. It is one of the greatest triumphs of humankind.

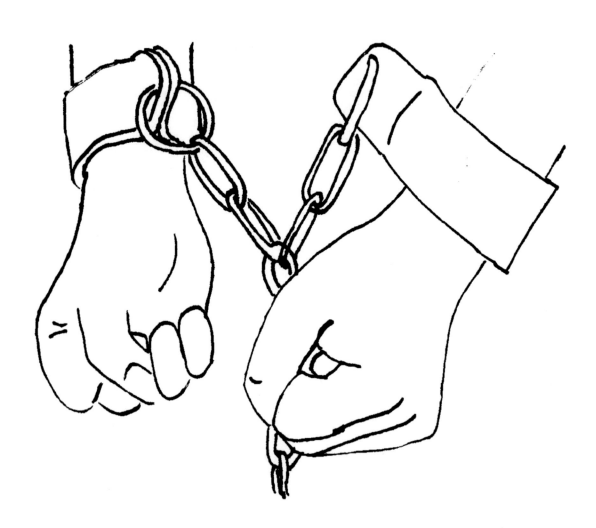

Slave Trade: Unit 3-14

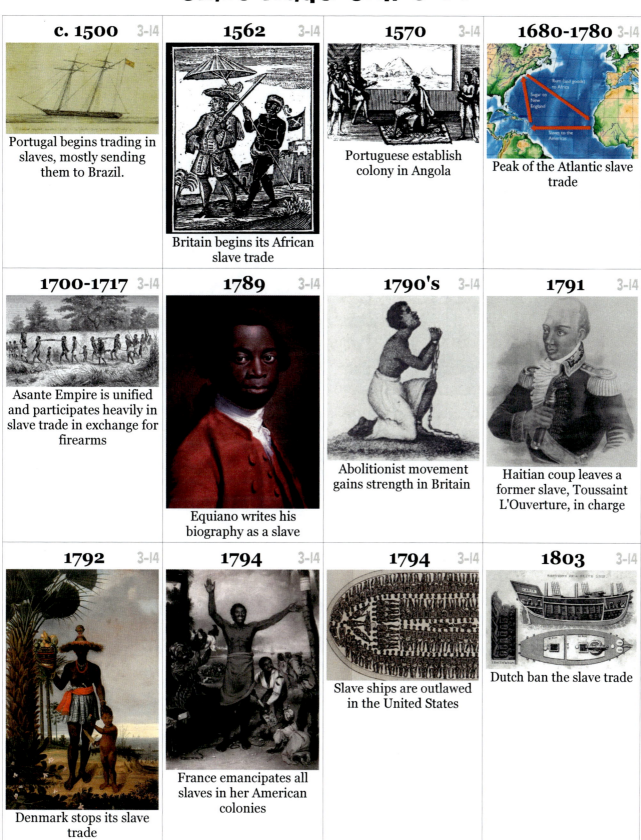

c. 1500 3-14

Portugal begins trading in slaves, mostly sending them to Brazil.

1562 3-14

Britain begins its African slave trade

1570 3-14

Portuguese establish colony in Angola

1680-1780 3-14

Peak of the Atlantic slave trade

1700-1717 3-14

Asante Empire is unified and participates heavily in slave trade in exchange for firearms

1789 3-14

Equiano writes his biography as a slave

1790's 3-14

Abolitionist movement gains strength in Britain

1791 3-14

Haitian coup leaves a former slave, Toussaint L'Ouverture, in charge

1792 3-14

Denmark stops its slave trade

1794 3-14

France emancipates all slaves in her American colonies

1794 3-14

Slave ships are outlawed in the United States

1803 3-14

Dutch ban the slave trade

1804   3-14

Slavery is illegal in the northern United States

1804   3-14

Black Republic formed in Haiti

1807   3-14

British ban the slave trade

1815   3-14

Britain pressures Spain and Portugal into signing a treaty to phase out the slave trade

1820   3-14

U.S. declares slave trade a form of piracy, punishable by death; U.S. Navy ships are dispatched to enforce this

1822   3-14

THE LOVE OF LIBERTY BROUGHT US HERE

REPUBLIC OF LIBERIA

African Colonization Society forms in the U.S. to create a Free Republic in Africa (Liberia, est. 1847) for freed former slaves

1831   3-14

Slave revolt breaks out in Jamaica and is brutally suppressed; leading to swift emancipation by British parliament in England

1833   3-14

Britain emancipates its West Indian slaves

1836   3-14

Portugal bans the slave trade

1839   3-14

Death of Capt. Ferrer, the Captain of the Amistad, July, 1839.

Amistad revolt erupts into new discussions on the legality and morality of slavery in the U.S.

1865   3-14

Slavery is illegal throughout all of the United States

1888   3-14

Slavery is illegal throughout the Americas

Triangular Trade

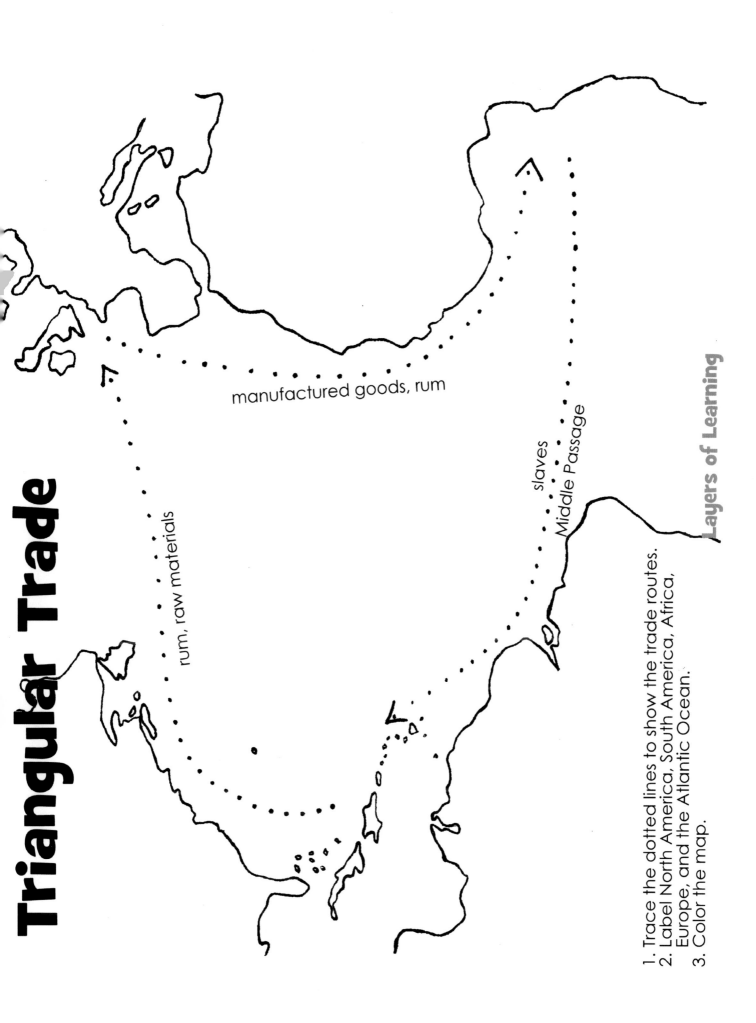

manufactured goods, rum

rum, raw materials

slaves
Middle Passage

1. Trace the dotted lines to show the trade routes.
2. Label North America, South America, Africa, Europe, and the Atlantic Ocean.
3. Color the map.

William Wilberforce

Cut out the curved arms and the rectangle with William Wilberforce on it. Color the craft and write quotes from Wilberforce in each of the lined spaces. Fold the long rectangle along the solid lines to form a box, gluing the tab to the back of the last box. Glue the curved arms to the back of Wilberforce. Make two small paper chains to place in Wilberforce's hands. On the links of the chain write down the evils of slavery. Glue the paper chains, one in each hand. This represents Wilberforce breaking the chains of slavery.

William Wilberforce

Brazil

Brazil's Flag

Auriverde means _____.

The gold represents_____.

The green represents_____.

The blue globe in the center shows a night sky with _____ stars, each one representing _____.

The 27 stars are arranged to pattern the night sky on November 15th, 1889, the day that Brazil was made a _____.

The band across the globe says "Ordem e Progresso" which means _____.

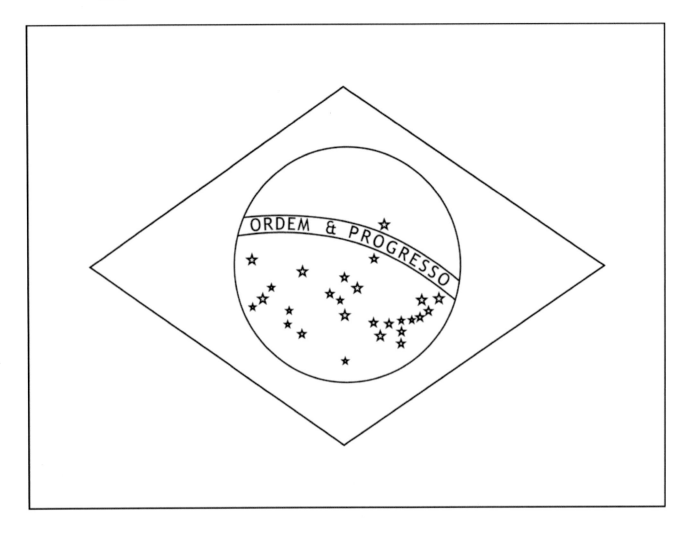

Identification Flowchart For Common Minerals

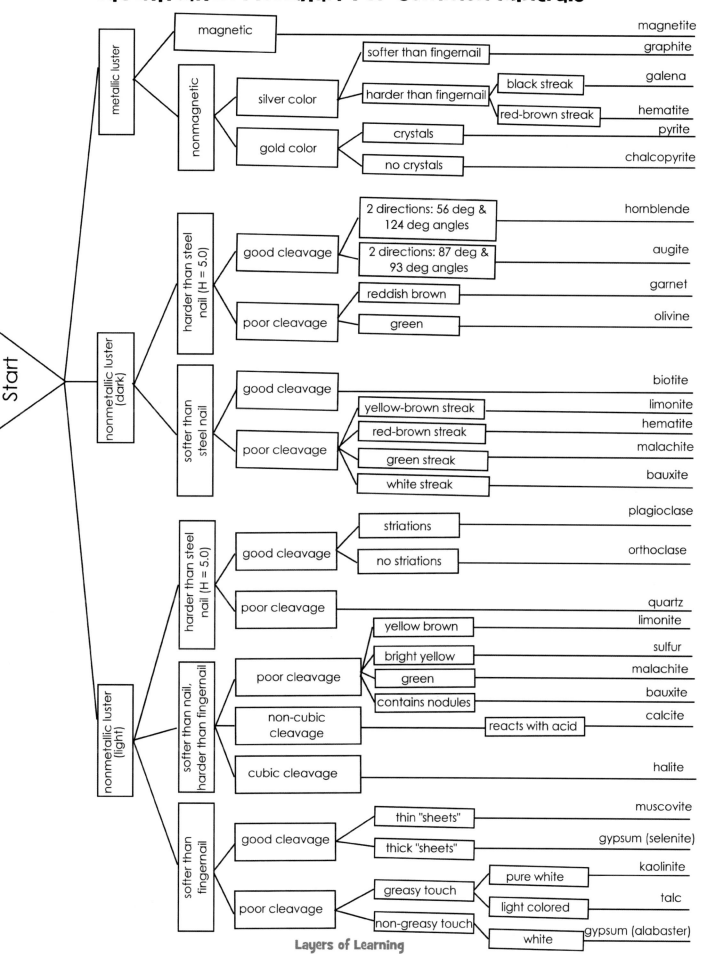

Start

metallic luster
- magnetic → magnetite
- nonmagnetic
  - silver color
    - softer than fingernail → graphite
    - harder than fingernail
      - black streak → galena
      - red-brown streak → hematite
  - gold color
    - crystals → pyrite
    - no crystals → chalcopyrite

nonmetallic luster (dark)
- harder than steel nail (H = 5.0)
  - good cleavage
    - 2 directions: 56 deg & 124 deg angles → hornblende
    - 2 directions: 87 deg & 93 deg angles → augite
  - poor cleavage
    - reddish brown → garnet
    - green → olivine
- softer than steel nail
  - good cleavage → biotite
  - poor cleavage
    - yellow-brown streak → limonite
    - red-brown streak → hematite
    - green streak → malachite
    - white streak → bauxite

nonmetallic luster (light)
- harder than steel nail (H = 5.0)
  - good cleavage
    - striations → plagioclase
    - no striations → orthoclase
  - poor cleavage → quartz
- softer than nail, harder than fingernail
  - poor cleavage
    - yellow brown → limonite
    - bright yellow → sulfur
    - green → malachite
    - contains nodules → bauxite
  - non-cubic cleavage
    - reacts with acid → calcite
  - cubic cleavage → halite
- softer than fingernail
  - good cleavage
    - thin "sheets" → muscovite
    - thick "sheets" → gypsum (selenite)
  - poor cleavage
    - greasy touch
      - pure white → kaolinite
      - light colored → talc
    - non-greasy touch
      - white → gypsum (alabaster)

Layers of Learning

Mineral Scavenger Hunt

Go to the grocery store and find these foods that have important minerals within them. Check off each box as you find the mineral-rich food.

Mineral	Mineral-rich foods	FOUND IT!
Boron Boosts metabolism	Almonds	
	Carrots	
	Dates	
Calcium Makes bones and teeth strong	Cheese	
	Milk	
	Spinach	
Chromium Helps your body metabolize sugars	Broccoli	
	Barley	
	Oats	
Chlorine Helps with digestion	Salt	
	Cocoa powder	
Copper Improves enzyme function for metabolism	Mushrooms	
	Kale	
	Chocolate bar	
Iron Helps make red blood cells and keeps your muscles strong (including your heart)	Seafood	
	Meat	
	Eggs	
Manganese Helps bone, tissue, and cell growth	Pecans	
	Whole wheat bread	
	Kidney beans	
Selenium Supports your immune system so you can fight off disease	Sunflower seeds	
	Onions	
	Tuna fish	
Silicon Helps build cartilage and bone	Celery	
	Peppers	
	Potatoes	

Mohs Mineral Hardness Scale

Minerals are classified by how hard they are. A harder mineral can scratch a softer mineral. Use a scratch test to put sample minerals in order from softest to hardest.

Hardness	Mineral	Letter	A drawing or description of your sample
1	talc		
2	gypsum		
3	calcite		
4	fluorite		
5	apatite		
6	orthoclase		
7	quartz		
8	topaz		
9	corundum		
10	diamond		

Making Buttons in Colonial America

You are a buttoner, a button maker in the colonies. You don't want to make the same everyday buttons today though, so you decide to paint scenes on your buttons. Decorate each of these buttons in a unique and special way.

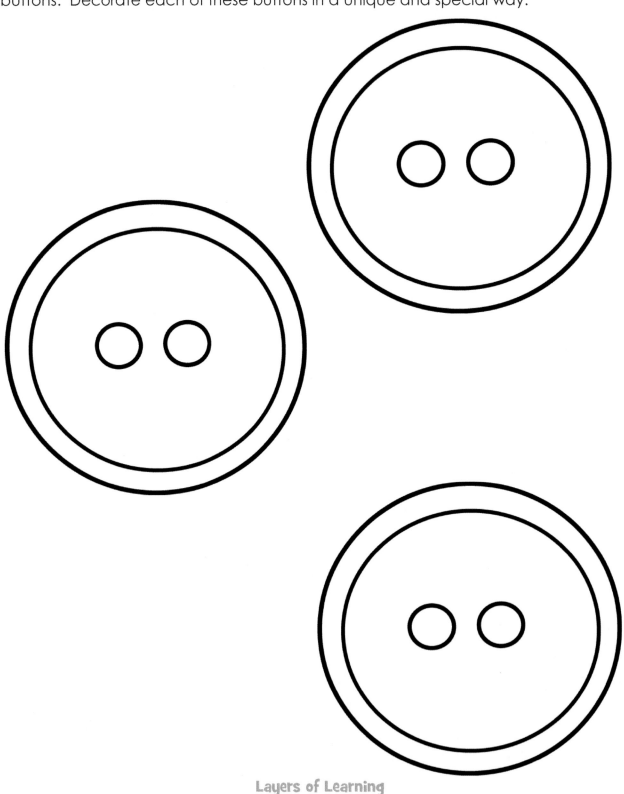

ABOUT THE AUTHORS

Karen & Michelle . . .
Mothers, sisters, teachers, women who are passionate
about educating kids.
We are dedicated to lifelong learning.

Karen, a mother of four, who has homeschooled her kids for more than eight years with her husband, Bob, has a bachelor's degree in child development with an emphasis in education. She lives in Utah where she gardens, teaches piano, and plays an excruciating number of board games with her kids. Karen is our resident Arts expert and English guru {most necessary as Michelle regularly and carelessly mangles the English language and occasionally steps over the bounds of polite society}.

Michelle and her husband, Cameron, homeschooling now for over a decade, teach their six boys on their ten acres in beautiful Idaho country. Michelle earned a bachelor's in biology, making her the resident Science expert, though she is mocked by her friends for being the *Botanist with the Black Thumb of Death*. She also is the go-to for History and Government. She believes in staying up late, hot chocolate, and a no whining policy. We both pitch in on Geography, in case you were wondering, and are on a continual quest for knowledge.

Visit our constantly updated blog for tons of free ideas,
free printables, and more cool stuff for sale:
www.Layers-of-Learning.com

Made in the USA
Middletown, DE
04 April 2025

73769634R00031